THE ART OF
THERAPY

THE ART OF
THERAPY

LOUIS EVERSTINE

Mental Research Institute

Library of Congress Control Number: 2012921162
ISBN: Hardcover   978-1-4797-4768-9
                Softcover   978-1-4797-4767-2
                Ebook   978-1-4797-4769-6

Indexed by Stephanie Ernestine Salera.
Reviewed by Hannah Lyn C. Creencia.
Text Preparation by Rana Soinski
Production Assistance by Tim Fitch, Kate Austria

This book was printed in the United States of America.

To order additional copies of this book, contact:
Xlibris Corporation
1-888-795-4274
www.Xlibris.com
Orders@Xlibris.com
115581

For Diana, angel of my mornings

TABLE OF CONTENTS

I. Primary Colors

II. Perspectives

PREFACE

Until the age of forty, I had not thought of doing psychotherapy. I had been a teacher and researcher, so when I began seeing clients it was with a sense of wonder leavened by fear. With experience, I realized that I had been doing therapy throughout my life. As an adolescent and a young man, no trait was so natural to me as an ability to listen to people when they talked about themselves. To remain silent and pay attention to every word they had to say was a form of entertainment to me. Passive receptivity it surely was, but reflective contemplation just the same, as well as a fascination with the complexity of every human life. If you give yourself wholeheartedly to listening, you will never be bored.

Coming to the Mental Research Institute as cofounder of an emergency treatment service was a turning point in my development as a therapist. My wife, Diana Sullivan Everstine, and I directed a staff of practitioners and interns who made themselves available to calls for mental health assistance at any hour of the day or night. A majority of those calls came from police officers who had been summoned to the homes of people in distress and who were turning their cases over to us for in-home services. When our workers, usually a man and a woman, arrived at the home, the police would leave. Many an intervention was conducted in living rooms or at kitchen tables. Many clients, although in dire distress, would offer coffee.

With the valuable assistance of our friend Arthur Bodin and local county funding, we kept the Emergency Treatment Center going for about fifteen years. Eventually, with the shifting sands of bureaucratic priorities, funding was withdrawn, leaving only brick-and-mortar clinics. Since then, we have devoted ourselves to private practice for forty years.

At this writing, I have in my practice clients who were born in China and India and Germany and France and Lebanon and Russia and Sri Lanka. They speak the universal language of anxiety and depression, etc., and continuously remind me that people are everywhere the same in any valuable aspect, even though they suffer the common delusion that differences in culture make for differences in human nature. Nevertheless, once the language barrier is crossed and differing customs accepted, the focus of the dialogue can be on similarities. There is no ethnic therapy.

Those of us who have the arrogance to take up this profession are often in need of a compass as a guide, so that we and those who come to us asking to be changed do not lose our way. This book is not a manual or curriculum or template or system or formula or PowerPoint that would insult the reader's intelligence, but instead a set of general principles that may inform the therapy experience. Because it would be naive to assume that two courses of treatment would follow the same path, this means that no therapist can operate according to a single theory or one-size-fits-all intervention. We have had our Jungians and Adlerians and Rogerians and Ericksonians and followers of countless other gurus, and today much of their wisdom has expired. And since each client is unique, therapy must necessarily be free-form, spontaneous to participation, situation, and event. No two cases are alike.

Few of the helping professions are unique in both concept and intention. Ours is one of those. It functions without formula, equipment, fixed agenda, or the trappings of an office with more than two chairs as furniture. What does it amount to in the end? Nothing more nor less than helping people straighten out their lives. So be it.

When a magician retires, hanging up his coat with the inside pockets for the last time, he may decide to write a book in which he describes the illusions he has used to charm people these many years. These are my illusions.

ACKNOWLEDGMENTS

In three decades as a clinician, I have made the acquaintance of and enjoyed the company of many colleagues who served as rich sources of inspiration. Among them are Andie Knutson and Richard Seiden at Berkeley; Roy Hamlin, Bill Bendig, and John Barry at Pittsburgh; Art Bodin and John Weakland at MRI; and Murray Tondow at the California School of Professional Psychology. I am grateful, as well, to the kind folks who invited Diana and me to their clinics and conferences to give lectures and workshops, namely Anne Ancelin-Schutzenberger and Pierre and Sylvie Angel and Catherine Mesnard in France, Guy Maruani in Belgium, Wanda Badura-Madej in Poland, Bert van Luyn and Herman Vergouwen in Holland, Maestro Felipe Gutierrez in Mexico, and Bjorn Reigstad and Knut Sorgaard in Norway. The titles and meetings of these visits, from north of the Arctic Circle to southern Mexico, are lost in memory, but the hospitality of those gracious hosts is not.

At MRI, I found a role model in the incomparable Paul Watzlawick, who, after the death of Don Jackson, became the face of the institute in this country and abroad. His wry humor was never in short supply, and much in display in books such as *How Real Is Real?*, *How to Make Yourself Miserable*, and *Ultrasolutions*. Paul wrote forewords to two of Diana's and my books, and greatly admired the two dogs that we took with us when working at MRI. One incident in particular casts light on his personality. I once asked him to write a letter of reference for a job to which I was applying. He said, "Let's do it the Austrian way. You write the letter and I'll sign it." This master clinician has gone to the lecture hall in the sky, but we never knew such a "hail fellow well met."

PROLOGUE

Sigmund Freud returned to life recently. He landed in Vienna, where he visited the current tenants of his apartment in the Berggasse, and went to a picnic given in his honor at a local park by some of his great-grandchildren. After a brief visit to London, he traveled on to Worchester, Massachusetts, where in 1909 he had given a series of lectures at Clark University. A television reporter caught up with him there and recorded this interview.

CNN: You've been dead these seventy-three years. When you came back to life, what was it that most surprised you?

FREUD: As you know, the last time I was alive it was in England. The council there has seen fit to retire those two-story buses that I loved so much. I didn't drive, so Martha and I would ride them everywhere.

CNN: Since you came to the States, have you seen local newspapers?

FREUD: No, I only watch your channel to get the latest.

CNN: Have recent events appalled you?

FREUD: Not at all. I foresaw much of this in my *Civilization and Its Discontents*.

CNN: Have people taken that book's teachings to heart?

FREUD: No, indeed they haven't. People have made no progress in expressing their pent-up anger outwardly; instead, they turn it upon themselves and call it "depression." I am sad to say that today, as I wrote then, people are too civilized for their own good.

CNN: And therapy, has it changed?

FREUD: Since I invented psychoanalysis, a hundred forms of therapy have evolved, many of them in a deliberate attempt to discredit me. As you know, I still am widely disliked—the prophet without honor, and so on.

CNN: Surely you are honored by your many imitators.

FREUD: Not enough. My "talking cure" has been replaced by a bagful of tricks. Someone gave me a book about these snake-oil "treatments" by a wonderful lady called Margaret Singer. She tells about clowns who try to help people by waving a finger in their faces. Someone else tries to make the person behave like a baby; others give the person a piece of candy whenever he or she says something "healthy." As a young man, I admired Lincoln, who said, "You can fool some of the people some of the time"—you know that one.

CNN: Didn't you try hypnosis with your clients?

FREUD: Yes, and I gave up on it early in my career. The hypnotic state has nothing to do with reality.

CNN: Is reality training an important component of therapy?

FREUD: Every effort of the therapist is an attempt to induce people to confront their own reality, which has become distorted, unfortunately, by self-delusion.

CNN: How do you see the future of therapy?

FREUD: Its importance cannot be discounted, of course. The rigid rules have been relaxed, and that may be a good thing. For example, the consulting room ambience in which the client reclines in a couch with the therapist seated at the end, out of the client's line of sight, was a silly contrivance that I now regret. It symbolized one person's dominance and the other's submission. The term "patient" says volumes. One must *be* patient as a condition of being cured.

CNN: In other words, a client must wait until the doctor can work his or her magic—a classic "one down" situation.

FREUD: That's right. Another thing: lifetime therapy has no place in this century. I kept my clients for many years because, quite frankly, I needed the money early in my career; later on, I did it out of habit. Perhaps feeling guilty, I dealt with this subject in my monograph, "Analysis Terminable and Interminable," but no one paid attention.

CNN: We're nearly out of time. Thank you so much, Dr. Freud, for your agreeing to this interview. I know that there will be many demands on your time for public appearances. Would you like a farewell word to our audience?

FREUD: Yes. Goodnight, Martha, wherever you are.

INTRODUCTION

Psychotherapy is a relationship between a therapist and a client or clients, whose purpose is to solve the client's problem or problems. The nature of the relationship is the key to therapeutic success, in that rapport is essential. One could say that therapy is the second oldest profession, because it involves talking with a person for a fee.

Above all, therapy is an art, not a science. On this point not even therapists agree. For example, psychiatry makes little pretense about being based on research other than drug trials. By contrast, psychology contains a cadre of academics who suffer from the delusion that what happens in therapy can be catalogued and quantified. Some of the more radical proponents of this folly even believe they can write a manual that a therapist can follow step by step in conducting a therapy session. Freud, who made no claim of being a scientist after he left neurology, would be appalled.

The role of science is to find out the secrets of the universe, to answer questions about how the world works. In its own niche, the scientific study of people seeks to identify broad principles of human personality and motivation, and since Wilhelm Wundt opened the first laboratory of its kind in 1879, psychological research has contributed mightily to our understanding of people in general.

By contrast, therapy is an intimate encounter in which a client is the center of the universe, so to speak. He or she asks nothing more than the full attention of the therapist. In turn, the therapist strives to give a client the full benefit of his or her knowledge and experience—the art. There are no templates, no guidelines, to govern a course of therapy. Its twists and turns are essentially spontaneous, because there is no one like the client and no one has identical problems.

As an art form, there are as many therapies as there are therapists. There are also as many "schools," each with its own concepts and methods, as there are therapists who desire to belong to a "school." (It's a comfort to many to "belong" to something. There are those who still say, with pride, things like "I'm an Adlerian.") Doctrines of therapeutic practice, so to speak, can be grouped into two main types: one would rearrange the person's thoughts and the other would help the person to gain greater control of his or her emotions. The label "cognitive" can be applied to the first, and "emotional intelligence" to the second.

Schools of therapy are like the heads of Hydra; for each one abandoned, a new one appears. Psychiatrists seldom flit from one to the other, rigidly focused as they are on the belief that the right prescription can fix any problem. By contrast, psychologists are absurdly faddish. They are constantly on the lookout for the latest technique that will help make their work easier, often leading them to worship a new guru in the process; just having a guru is reassuring to some. A logical extension of this quest for labor-saving methods is the delusion that a method should be called a "treatment."

An unfortunate legacy of therapy's origin in medicine is the belief that for each diagnosis there is a standard form of treatment or treatments (not to mention the chimera of "cure"). For dehydration there is saline solution; for a bee sting, an injection of Benadryl; for cancer, radiation or chemotherapy. Nevertheless, human psychological problems do not lend themselves to treatments, nor in fact to any textbook palliatives. Problems arise from interactions between and among people, and will only be alleviated by new interactions—such as those between therapist and client—and new ways of behaving in existing relationships. The medical model cannot be applied to therapy, which in its essential form is pure conversation. As we all know, conversation is fluid and unpredictable, and obeys few rules save that of politesse.

Just because therapy obeys no rules and, done properly, "goes with the flow" of conversation, it resists strict training techniques. Because there can be no definitive training manual and methods cannot be quantified, learning to do therapy well relies more on life experience as its teacher. Being of sound mind, an agreeable disposition, and having attained a certain age are key ingredients in the making of a helpful therapist. And therapists are certainly made, not born. The sole genetic marker of a likely therapist is the gene of being a good listener; that virtue can't be taught.

We can take some lessons from therapies gone awry, failed systems that may have flowered briefly but were found wanting and abandoned before too much damage was done. An instructive guide to systems such as these is the book by Margaret Singer and Janja Lolich, in which a host of questionable or fraudulent or plainly deranged theories of therapy are revealed, critiqued, and debunked as travesties on the profession. Examples from the book include:

1. Regressing the client to the moment of birth, providing a "primary mother" who will re-parent the person
2. Convincing the client that he or she lived at a previous time and has returned through reincarnation
3. Convincing the client that spirits of people who have died have invaded the person and are causing his or her problems; for this malady, one is said to require the services of a "channeler"
4. Instilling the belief that the client has been abducted by aliens who are the sources of current conflicts;
5. Confrontation of the client by a therapist or group members, often leading to verbal attacks or even the supposedly therapeutic "primal scream"
6. "Sexual healing"
7. The therapist's finger is repeatedly moved back and forth close to the client's eyes, thereby releasing bad memories

It would be possible to find humor in some of these aberrations were it not for the fact that one role of a therapist is to interpret reality to his or her client. To persuade a client to believe in any of these "therapies" is an appalling misuse of the power of transference (of which, more later). Of course, charlatans emerge wherever there is money to be made and "snake oil" to be sold. And yes, every art form has its Pollocks and Warhols and Dalis, but the harm that some of our colleagues have done to people is not to their aesthetic sensibilities but their peace of mind.

How is it that people are so gullible to fall for fairy dust merchants such as those unmasked by Singer and Lolich? It happens because of the nature of our profession and those who practice it. When a critic accuses us of "playing God," we dismiss it as a cliché, and when we say it among ourselves we consider it a facetious remark. In fact, the phrase is instructive and worth thinking about because it identifies both a blessing and a curse on our role as caregivers. Our clients come forward asking to be changed in some way. They confer upon us the gift of their trust. Many are willing to share intimate details of their lives, past and present. Moreover, they pay us for the privilege.

Because clients have such a need to suspend their disbelief when they come to us for help, they *want* us to be authoritative without being authoritarian, self-confident without being self-serving, critical without being punitive. This is a powerful force that, as we have seen, can be misused and even perverted. The dependence that leads people to be conned by false therapies is the other side of the coin of transference—the subject of another chapter.

In summary, the thesis of this book is that therapy is no more or less than a dialogue between a person who seeks help and a professional person who seeks to help. No less than that, because it concerns vital issues in the person's life; no more than that because the therapist offers not rules but advice. Further, therapy is not a scientific discipline, nor can its vital attributes be quantified in any way. Therapy does, in fact, concern itself often with social mores, and thus often deals with moral principles, even though having no connection with religious dogma. It is an art, pure and simple, both enjoying and suffering the spontaneity of art. Its value lies in the eye of the beholder—the client. In practical terms, if the therapeutic experience "works" for the client, it is good therapy.

I. PRIMARY COLORS

1. ESTABLISHING RAPPORT

Freud discovered transference in 1892, according to his biographer, Ernest Jones.[1] It happened when a woman client, at the end of a session, seized Freud in a passionate embrace; he was only "saved" when a servant entered the room. Soon after this incident, Freud came to the realization that ". . . therapeutic improvement was dependent on the personal relationship between patient and physician."[2] This incident and Freud's discovery teach the lessons that one should never underestimate a client, and that the relationship formed in therapy is a powerful bond. In time, Freud concluded that there can be no successful therapy unless transference occurs. It is a form of unrequited love that a therapist must treat with extreme sensitivity and manage deftly. Rapport with the client[3] is an essential starting point for the therapy experience.

Establishing rapport, of course, begins at the moment of first meeting the client. But therapists are universally handicapped by the need to obtain identifying information about clients at the outset. If the case will be paid for at least in part by an insurance company, a series of numbers such as birth date, authorization code, etc., must be collected as soon as possible. And if the therapist has a billing clerk, that person will likely insist that this information be collected at the first meeting. One way to do this is to greet the client in the waiting room, introduce oneself, and ask if he or she would mind filling out a form; the therapist will leave and return shortly. This first encounter thereby becomes a straightforward business transaction, routinely devoid of emotion and the gravity of the therapeutic relationship. After a few minutes, the therapist will show the client to the office, along the way offering coffee or tea or water. When the client is seated and given something to drink if requested, the therapist can ask whether or not the client has visited a therapist previously; if so, it may be politic to ask if the prior experience was useful. Following these pleasantries, the search for rapport can begin.

At some time during the first session, the therapist can open the subject of the confidentiality protections that are due to the client. By law, a client has the right ("privilege" in the letter of the law) to have the proceedings of therapy sessions kept secret.[4] In fact, his or her very participation in therapy is protected by absolute confidentiality. In real terms, this principle applies when a therapist receives a telephone call or e-mail inquiry such as "I understand that John Smith is seeing you for psychotherapy; may I get some information from you about him?" The therapist, in turn, should say something like this: "If I know John Smith professionally, and if he gives me permission to talk to you, I'll call you back. What's your number?" Naturally, the confidentiality rule applies equally to written records of the client's identity, role as a client, and the contents of therapy sessions. (This subject will be examined again later.).

There are, of necessity, mandated exceptions to the rights of clients to confidentiality. For example, if he or she threatens to harm another person, the therapist is required to warn the threatened person and to inform the police of the threat. (Practically speaking, police will likely do nothing except to make a record of the information.) Suspected child or elder abuse must be revealed to whatever local agency is charged with helping victims of abuse. Case law concerning making reports of a threat of suicide is often contradictory; in practice, however, a therapist is constrained to do whatever would reasonably be necessary to keep the client alive. Both rights and exceptions can be perplexing, and will probably delay the useful work of therapy while being presented and discussed. For that reason, a brief oral summary for the client may suffice, followed by a written handout given at the end of the session, inviting reflection at home. The subject is presented here because when carefully explained these laws and protective procedures may be reassuring to the client and even contribute to the establishment of rapport.

Once the necessary formalities have been duly discharged, the interaction between therapist and client can focus on some basic building blocks of acquaintance, such as, what is your profession? Are you planning to continue working at your company (agency, business, etc.) until retirement age? Who is living with you at home? These are outwardly innocuous questions that can lead into finding out about the client's personal history. They are most appropriate when a client is reticent and there is a need to draw him or her out of a shell formed by fear or shyness. Conversely, when a client is forthcoming it will be wise to let the narrative proceed without interruption; details of the history can be drawn out in subsequent sessions.

Vital information to be obtained in the first meeting includes the client's support group, a sort of inventory of friends and family. One needs to know the names of the core family members and their roles in the family constellation. The most important aspect of this data-gathering process is that the names must be stored in memory by the therapist for future reference, if necessary by taking notes in the first session. (Note-taking will be discussed in the next chapter.)

Throughout the early stages of therapy, and probably sooner than later, the therapist will form an opinion about the nature of the problem that motivated the client to seek help. Full knowledge of this resides with the client, of course, and ideally it will be expressed by him or her spontaneously. The better the rapport, the more readily will the client trust, and with trust comes a willingness to reveal the dilemma or loss or crisis or conflict or general sense of helplessness that led the person to your office. This orienting disclosure is a necessary component of trust-building. The problem or problems as stated by the client must be accepted at face value and without judgment. (If the true problem is later found to have been hidden, hiding it is a primary problem.) A stated problem may seem trivial or even ludicrous to the therapist, but it has preoccupied the thoughts of the client for some time, in most cases; and to that person it has become overwhelming. It must be acknowledged and validated as a genuine threat to wellbeing. When you ask yourself what could happen to motivate you to seek your own therapy, you can get in touch with feelings like what your client felt before finding your name in the telephone directory. Your empathy toward these feelings and your acceptance of their causes will contribute to establishing rapport early in therapy.

In summary, rapport is a vital ingredient in therapy and must occur before serious therapeutic work can start. An impediment is the unfortunate chore of collecting data for billing purposes. A frank discussion of provisions for the security of client information, as well as the limits of client confidentiality, may build trust if conducted sensitively. Gradually, the client will provide information about feelings toward his or her current job, the roles of the people who inhabit his or her life, and a rough projection of his or her plans for the future. These revelations are best received by the therapist without critical comment, because they contribute to the process of making the client feel at home in the therapy environment. As this feeling of wellbeing evolves, the client can be expected to describe the life events that led him or her to seek the safe haven of therapy. When rapport exists, both partners will know it.

2. LISTENING

From the point of view of a client, the therapist should not forget what he or she has been told. The abundant personal information provided by a client in the first session, sometimes revealed against the client's better judgment, should have been retained and needn't be reiterated. For this, a brief intake note written after the session will suffice. This note should contain facts such as the client's type of work, time on the job, the names of key persons such as the spouse or partner, and the ages of any children; these data will be useful to the therapist for reference later on. (The presenting problem should be fully recalled by the therapist and require no documentation.) That this much stored information suffices opens the question of what written notes, in general, should contain. First, a clear distinction should be drawn between these intake notes and process notes as described below.

If you've seen one of the ubiquitous hospital shows on TV, you've noticed that in scenes when a patient is being wheeled into the emergency room, nurses and other attendants are hovering around, taking notes as a doctor calls out data about vital signs, etc. Keeping copious records of a patient's condition at key intervals is intrinsic to hospital care. Even in a routine visit to a general practitioner's office, note-taking and chart entry are standard procedures. Seldom are these records challenged for accuracy or thought to have been taken inappropriately. Medical doctors make and store notes, and their colleagues in psychiatry do the same. Sigmund Freud himself established the habit, and the familiar image of him sitting at the end of a chaise on which lies a client, while Freud writes in a notebook, is well ingrained.

The difficulty with this procedure, which has become standard practice and has not been examined in terms of its significance, is that psychiatric information is qualitatively different from information of the strictly medical kind. It involves personal relationships, likes and dislikes, ambitions and fantasies, and often, openly pathological lines of thought. These facts about a person are obviously more sensitive than those representing, e.g., blood sugar level or fallen arches. Few people would oppose details of a gall bladder operation or repair of a broken arm being entered into a chart bearing their names. By contrast, mental health information has inherent hazards.

Many psychiatrists, psychologists, and marriage counselors have never visited a courtroom; if they had, they would be aware of its affinity to scenes depicted in *Alice in Wonderland*. (Humpty Dumpty says, "When I use a word . . . it means just what I choose it to mean—neither more nor less.") The purpose of a trial is to obtain, examine, and make decisions based on facts as proven, and facts alone. To accomplish that, a judge has virtually unlimited powers to admit or deny the admittance of proffered evidence. In practical terms, mental health records are admissible on the mere whim of a judge, and shrewd attorneys are not shy about using this to their clients' advantage. The point of this detour into the judicial process is that the most intimate observations about, or quotations from, a therapy client can be made public, and often are. Therefore, a therapist can best be bound by this principle: if you believe that permitting your records concerning a client to be read aloud in open court might be detrimental to the client, do not record them.[1]

There is more than one way to take process notes without exposing a client to risk. For example, what you write may take the form of an account of what you, the therapist, did in the course of a therapy session: "Asked her about her adoptive parents"; "Counseled him to offer accompanying his wife to mass once each month"; "Discussed the value of exercising often at a gym"; "Administered personality inventory"; "Suggested that he see a psychiatrist to be evaluated for medication." In this way, a record is being kept and duly dated; it will fully serve the need for a therapist to recall what occurred during a previous session, and it will confound the ability of any outsider to eavesdrop on the inner sanctum. This is not what Freud had in mind, but no one ever subpoenaed his process notes, and he would not recognize the present "open society" in which almost anyone can find out things about almost anyone.[2] For reasons that will soon be clear, notes in any form should be written after, not during, therapy.

Among the reasons that note-taking is problematic is that it requires the therapist to look at a piece of paper instead of the client. When Freud sat at the head of the chaise, he was protected from the client's gaze, undoubtedly from reasons unique to his personality.[3] In the approach to therapy advocated here, a therapist should look the client in the eye, without staring, as often and as long as possible during a session. This is one way in which the client can be assured that the therapist is listening to him or her.

Just as knowledge of perspective and proportion are essential to drawing or painting, listening is the *sine qua non* of a therapist's art. Active listening is only conveyed by the nonverbal cues of attentiveness, of which looking directly at the person is one. Body position is another: arms should not be crossed, for example, and the orientation of the therapist's body should be open toward the client. A desk should not create a symbolic barrier between the two, a vase of flowers should not block the view of one person to the other, and objects should not be handled distractedly. A therapist should not hide behind a notebook or anything else.

A key question that owes everything to the context in which it should be asked is: "Have you thought of doing something to hurt yourself?" There are times during a therapy session when a client's mood will suddenly darken and a look of sadness crosses the client's face. Times like these call upon a therapist's deepest reserves of empathy; they must be met with concern and an attempt to console. When the mood has passed, there will be an opportunity to find out how pervasive the sadness is by asking that question. If the answer implies serious suicidal thoughts, it may be considered a cry for help, and therapy should be restructured to the primary goal of keeping the person alive. When a genuine threat is heard, a therapist can ask the client for a promise to call him or her if a thought of suicide occurs again. When the client makes a specific promise such as this, the "contract" is complete; there is no need to belabor the issue. By accepting this promise, a therapist reinforces the bond of trust, because he or she has taken the client's word on a subject of extreme importance to their relationship. On life-and-death matters, a therapist should be ready to be the first person called in the crisis moment. Even so, the wise therapist will be aware that even a written "no-suicide contract" is no guarantee, nor is an oral promise a substitute for continued monitoring of the lethality of the situation.

In summary, rapport, once established, must be maintained. An opportunity to make sure of this occurs whenever the client brings emotion to the therapy process. Whether the emotion is positive or negative, a therapist must acknowledge and accept the emotion at face value. Creative listening enhances rapport, and is best expressed by eye contact. Note-taking poses a risk to rapport because it raises the confidentiality issue. Therapy notes are only an aide-mémoire for the therapist's benefit, and what is entered should protect—not expose—the client. A crisis fraught with both danger and opportunity arises when a client threatens suicide. If it happens, the therapy relationship is irrevocably changed. Nevertheless, a therapist can find in the threat a sign of trust on the client's part. A caring response will only strengthen the relationship.

3. FINDING OUT

As therapists, we owe our clients many varieties of care, not least of which are establishing trust, listening carefully, remembering key events and people in their lives, as well as protecting them from the insensitivity of bureaucrats and the greed of plaintiffs' attorneys. We are asked by our clients to help them make significant changes in their lives, to improve their welfare, and in general, enable them to feel better about themselves. We achieve these goals by giving them practical advice about how to solve the problems that press them in the moment, or increase their understanding of events from the past that still affect them unfairly.

When we have deeply inquired into the circumstances of a client's life, we can begin to appreciate more of his or her *modus vivendi*, or way of living. Information is the means to discover the person's weaknesses in adjusting to his or her environment, and more importantly, the person's strengths. Some of this can be done by employing a series of probing questions set in nonthreatening terms. They should be asked at random intervals, and if they do not serve to open a dialogue on the subject, the therapist should quickly move on.

"What has been the most significant moment in your life until now?"

"If you were assured that you could not fail, what would you attempt to do during your lifetime?"

"What do you plan to be doing, and where will you be living five years [ten years] from now?"

"Did something bad happen to you when you were younger?"

"If you could wave a magic wand, what would you change about your life today?"

"Who has been the most important person in your life until now?"

"What is the most-valued personal achievement of your life until now?"

Far from rhetorical, questions such as these, if answered candidly and followed by in-depth discussion, can provide useful insights into the client's inner world. They should be interspersed strategically when the conversation needs to change direction.

Using another approach, one can propose a hypothetical situation to explore how the partners in a relationship feel about each other; e.g., if a wife is the client, one can point to an empty chair and ask, "If your husband were here, what would he say if I asked him 'What is wrong with this lady, your wife?'" This hypothetical question can also be asked in a situation in which a close friend is an antagonist. "If your friend were here, what would he [she] say if asked, 'What is wrong with my client here?'" The answer to a question such as this reveals both the client's perception of the antagonist, and in many cases, an insight into how the relationship works or doesn't work.

An altogether different approach, also using a hypothetical situation, should only be used sensitively. When the client is bedeviled by an oppressive relationship, for example with his or her father, he or she can be asked, "If your father died in an accident, would you attend his funeral?" If the answer is yes, ask, "Would you cry?" The same hypothetical can be used when a rejecting lover has ruined a relationship, or a vindictive sister has poisoned the minds of the family against your client. In this way, the relationships that are to be healed can be identified and examined.

Taken one step further, a client can be asked, for example, "If the judge issued an order saying that you must file for divorce by the end of this month, what would you do?" (Of course this is an imaginary judge, but the implied premise of the question is that defiance of a court order could lead to jail.) By extension, one could ask, "If your medical doctor told you, sincerely, that he or she would not be responsible for your health if you did not quit your job by the end of the month, what would you do?" Questions such as these, farfetched as they may seem, contain a humorous element but may elicit answers that are helpful in understanding the client. They serve to clarify aspects of the person's value system that will act as guidelines for future interventions.

Psychological testing can yield insightful information as well. While many clinicians object to giving tests because they take time away from therapy sessions, their utility is not in question, and major insurance companies pay for the time. The best thing about test results is that they supply shortcuts to finding out aspects of the client's personality that might otherwise take hours of intensive interview to obtain. As an example, a quick, richly informative source of data is the Sentence Completion instrument devised by Julian Rotter many years ago and copied by many since. Confronted with the beginnings of sentences, the client is asked to finish them with words and phrases that reflect inner thoughts. The product is more than fifty statements that can be the subject of a many-faceted discussion with the client.

A very useful, even easier-to-administer objective test is the Coopersmith Inventory, a measure of self-esteem named for its creator. Norms and percentile ranks are provided for various age groups. If you have occasion, for instance, to tell a client that his or her self-esteem is at the fifth percentile in contrast to people of the same age, the reaction to this news will speak volumes about the person, and will open vital new lines of dialogue for therapy. Did the client expect the outcome, or is he or she shocked by the result? The next step is to take each of the test responses that *lowered* the score and inquire about why he or she answered that way.

Even therapists who do not rely on psychological testing will know and appreciate the reputation of the MMPI-2 as a diagnostic instrument. It has the virtue of being an objective test, scored and interpreted by computer. This untouched-by-human-hands aspect makes it the gold standard for use in forensic work, as well as for disability and workers' compensation claims. Some scoring systems for the MMPI produce reports in both graphic and narrative forms, and one generates 160 separate scales, each measuring a unique trait. The narrative portion of the report is naturally the most used, and a diagnostic impression is included in most scoring systems.

A word about diagnoses: as mentioned in chapter 2, any scrap of information about a person can be commandeered by a court of law and made public at trial. This means that a diagnosis, especially one that is derived from an objective test, can be a ticking bomb for your client. If the label given by the test report might possibly show the client in a negative light—in particular one that reflects a common taboo—and if there is a chance that the client may become involved in a legal action, the best course to follow may be to use the information yourself and discard the report. After all, the results of a test are the property of the person who took the test. The privilege prevails until relinquished.

In the helping professions, from medicine in the emergency

room to welfare social work, the practitioner is expected by professional standards to find out as much as possible about the patient or client. In psychotherapy, we take this mandate as far as necessary, only stopping short of violating the client's privacy by revealing to your potential informant that the client is being treated by you—unless given permission to do so. This means that we do not seek information from, for example, the client's spouse unless permitted. Even so, in the case of a child in therapy it is ethical to confer with the child's parents if they are willing to discuss their child with you. In sum, we cannot collect too much information about our clients, but the methods of collection are circumscribed.

4. REMEMBERING

An actor in a play might have to remember a hundred lines of dialogue—not only his or her lines but also those of the other characters who provide the cues. A therapist should not have to ask the client to reiterate an account of personal history, except of course to gather more details about what was previously mentioned, or to gain a deeper understanding of the narrative itself. For example:

> Your family moved often when you were a child, each year for a while. What was that like for you?

> Your uncle Leo was an important person in your childhood. What kind of a person was he?

> You told me that your parents encouraged you to play the violin, hiring a teacher to come to your

house during several years. Why did your lessons stop?

You said that your younger sister was molested by your stepfather. How did the experience of learning about that affect you?

Jane was your best friend in high school. Are you still in touch with her?

You said that Larry, your boss at work for many years, was transferred recently. How do you feel about that?

Recalling the who, what, and when of your client's life before now is a hallmark of your listening skills, and when remembered accurately, are requisites of maintaining rapport.

Remembering vital details of the person's life can be a key ingredient in achieving one of the most rewarding experiences of the therapy process. It happens when some perception or insight or interpretation is acknowledged by the client saying, "Exactly." Especially if it occurs in the first session, and only if it comes from the client spontaneously, this remark represents a moment of truth. It shows the client's trust of the therapist and the therapy so far, and it reassures the therapist that he or she is on the right track. In short, if you hear "exactly" from your client, consider it a personal epiphany.

The importance of finding out about and remembering the client's constellation of relationships cannot be overemphasized. It is because of and within the context of those relationships that the real work of therapy will be done. In searching for the root causes of a client's problems, the best strategy is to examine the core relationships and what has happened in them and what is happening now. As an example of this approach in action, consider the task of helping a person overcome the debilitating effects of acute depression. The symptoms of depression are fueled by anger that can have no outward expression. This suppressed anger is intended for an external object (cruel parent, unfaithful spouse, ungrateful boss, et al.) but cannot be vented or converted into overt aggression. This emotion, often felt with the heat of rage, is blocked from its intended object by a symbolic barrier and turned inward. This "barrier" has been established over time by the terms of the malignant relationship, or in many cases, by the early inculcation of values such as "to be angry is wrong" or "fighting back makes matters worse" or "learn to accept your fate." He or she may come to feel that the abuse from the antagonist was "deserved" in some way and therefore to be accepted and forgotten. The result of this kind of thinking is that the one who hates becomes self-hating. The person now feels worthless, helpless to do anything about the feeling, unable to cope, trapped in negative emotions—in a word, depressed.

Anger turned inward produces self-hatred. In the ultimate depressive state, as is found in the backward patients of mental hospitals, the sufferers say such things as, "I'm no good." "You should take me out and shoot me." "I don't deserve to live." They have entered the kingdom of the damned, solely because they have never, to this day, found a way to release their angry feelings.

The subject of depression is not, except in passing, the subject of this book, but is included to demonstrate the interactional view of psychopathology that underlies and informs this approach to therapy. People become depressed when their relationships with others become poisoned by repressed anger. Therefore, when confronted by a client who reports depressive symptoms, a therapist is well-advised to examine each of the client's current relationships, and if necessary those ended in the past, to find out who is the intended recipient of the unexpressed anger. "Who has made you so angry?" "Who is responsible for the rage that you feel?"

When the antagonist of your client has been identified, interactional therapy can begin. In essence, the intervention has become the equivalent of couple's therapy, in which a dyad is the source of your client's distress. The relationship must be relieved of its anger and a new relationship established as an outcome of therapy.

Remembering, as a key element in therapy, is a function of concentrating on every detail of the critical relationship. It is in the details that the core of the conflict will be found. Each incident when there has been miscommunication between the two or in which their values have clashed or in which the actions of one partner have harmed or demeaned the other, etc., should be analyzed step by step to see what went wrong and work toward undoing it. Ask:

What happened between you? When?

How long did it last?

Were other people involved?

What did he (she) say?

How did you feel when he (she) said that?

How did the incident end?

What has been the result until now?

The behavior of each person should be noted and analyzed, and the feelings felt by each should be examined.

Therapy requires an inventory of the most significant relationship or relationships in the person's life, followed by dissection of the real-life events that produced distress using a response-by-response interpretation of the behavior of each participant. This approach has much in common with surgery, in which each step follows logically from the one before. For this to occur in therapy, remembering accurately is a key factor. Making the same interpretation more than once, or recommending the same intervention twice, is much to be avoided in therapy; any note about a session for the chart can prevent a lapse in memory. When the client enters the office, one should be aware of the significant events in his or her life. Remembering the first name of a beloved aunt would also be beneficial.

5. PROTECTING

An extension of the primitive stigma against people who are "mentally ill" is that someone must save them from themselves. A further extension is that "normal" people must save themselves from the mentally ill. We project from the fact that they are, by definition, unstable, and that they may well be dangerous. (They might "fly off the handle" or "lash out blindly" or lose control in some hurtful way.) Of course, the stigma originates in the mysterious nature of this illness—too many unknowns in the equation. Because we cannot understand why people become that way, our fantasies lead us further to believe that they could do anything without warning. In short, they are unnatural creatures, and thus to be feared. An unreal fear such as this is unseemly in a therapist and must be suppressed. After all, a clear perception of reality is our stock in trade.

A characteristic of the therapist is that he or she does not have an innate aversion to people who have mental problems;

this trait is essential to entering and remaining in the profession. Unhappily, people from other walks of life are less sanguine about the symptoms of mental distress. Among them are many legislators and judges, the very authorities who make and enforce the rules of therapy practice. Never having been asked in their professions to help a troubled person up close and personal to solve a complex problem of living, they lack the experience or the wisdom to set therapy standards; but they do.

This state of affairs notwithstanding, the therapist navigates a minefield of professional standards, ethical constraints, licensing regulations, laws and dictates of case law that more often hinder than facilitate the task of helping their clients. (For this we have to thank the crackpots who invent demented "therapies" such as those described in the introduction to this book.) Take for example the conflicting constraints of promised confidentiality versus compelled disclosure that were cited in Chapter 2. As a caregiver, every impulse of the therapist inclines him or her to protect client confidentiality, but if he or she bills an insurance company for fees, nothing will be paid unless the client's date of birth and Social Security number are revealed.

A word about diagnoses: health insurance companies, drug companies, and even lawyers love diagnoses, to which they can anchor their vague speculations on what it means to be psychologically ill. The DSM, by its own definition, is a nomenclature; not a description or analysis, but a labeling. As a labeling system, it is subject to questions of this sort: which came first, the label or the aliment? In one well-known example, drug companies have been accused of promoting the diagnoses ADD and ADHD solely for the purpose of selling Adderall and Ritalin.

Diagnoses as labels are arbitrarily chosen and named. For example, the psychiatrist director of publication for DSM-IV, a revision of DSM-III-R, is said to have told his staff to remove any trace of the words "neurosis" or "neurotic" because they were Freudian terms.

Of course, a label only causes trouble when it is attached, in a database, with other labels such as name, age, SSN, marital status, etc. The wise therapist is well-advised to create two diagnoses for the client, namely an official one as ambiguous as possible and a second that is confined to his or her memory bank. The guiding principle is the same as the one mentioned in Chapter 2 concerning psychotherapy notes: should your client's diagnosis be linked to the client's identity in a database or discussed and defined in an open court? Your own values may guide you to the thought that it is no one else's business.

A therapy session is like a birthday party—you never know how it will turn out. The participants each bring their own agendas, their needs and illusions, their plans and apprehensions. What if a client begins to cry during a session? After a respectful silence on the part of the therapist, followed by "I'm sorry I made you cry, please forgive me," nothing more is to be done until the person regains his or her composure. Thus begins an entirely new session in which the former topic of conversation will be put aside in favor of an attempt to comfort the client and lessen his or her embarrassment at having revealed an emotion that was formerly suppressed. The theme of the session becomes a gentle inquiry into the feelings that produced tears: "I don't like to see you so sad. What were we saying that touched a nerve?" If the question does now lead to a new direction, away from the emotion itself, it may be wise to end the session and ask for a new meeting soon. In any case, both client and therapist know that a rich new vein of discovery has been opened and might well be explored further at another session. However cruel it was to elicit tears, getting closer to the heart of the person's experience can yield benefits in the long run.

What if a client threatens suicide at some point in a session? If that happens, therapy itself must pause immediately. Whether credible or not, this cry for help may not be ignored. The session turns to a search for how genuine was the threat. Here is the acid test of transference. Standard wisdom requires the therapist to find out what means the person would use, etc., in suicide to assess "lethality" (unfortunate word). The next step, according to custom, is to ask the person to pledge not to do it as part of a "contract" with the therapist. (This contract has virtually no force, but may serve to lessen a clinician's liability in the event that a completed suicide is followed by a lawsuit.) In practice, the last thing your clients will tell you, if they sincerely plan to do it, is how they would do it. A facetious or elaborate answer to the question signals that the plan is a fantasy. The prevention of suicide will not depend upon either a pledge or a contract. It depends upon the successful discovery and analysis of the *causes* of a client's threat.

One reason for the superficiality of a contract may derive

from the prevailing taboo about suicide and suicide threats. Most people consider a suicidal gesture repugnant and an actual suicide as immoral, disgusting, stupid, or all three. This reaction is understandable when one considers that suicide by a person they know leaves a psychological wound that, they sense, will not heal soon.

The motive for killing oneself arises in a toxic relationship of the person's present or past. The relationship has deteriorated to a point of no return, masked by what may be a series of threats. The purpose of these threats is to send a message to at least one other person that the threatener's death will be blamed on the other person. This other person can best be identified as the intended "target" of the suicidal death. If the client dies by suicide, the target will be punished by feelings of guilt that potentially can never be dispelled. One person is willing to trade life for the emotional destruction of another—"He drove her to suicide." Hatred so primitive as this has inspired our myth of a devil who personifies evil.

When a suicidal person sits across from you in the consulting room, try to imagine how the person could build up so much rage. What was done to him or her that would make it seem worthwhile to throw away life to ruin the life of someone else? The answer to this question begs the question, who is the intended target of this pathological anger? "Who *else* is involved?" is invariably asked when one makes use of the interactional view to explain behavior. In this example, what relationship has become so malignant that your client has arrived at only one possible solution?

There are cases in which the suicide threatener has been so manipulated that revenge against a person who is no longer in his or her life is unthinkable. The perpetrator could have been an abusive parent, a molester who was never punished, an adolescent bully—in effect, a ghost who haunts from the past. In the present, it could be an unfaithful spouse, a tyrannical boss, a "sworn enemy," a vindictive sibling, or anyone else whose slights or intimidation or betrayal have brought the person to the brink of retaliation by the only means left.[1]

When the therapist has identified the principal antagonist in the client's life, discovery of the nature of the relationship––present or past––begins. Your job is to protect the person from himself by defusing the anger that has contaminated the key relationship. (It might be more than one person, such as "the people at work" or "my family" or "his family" or "her family." Even so, there is usually a "private enemy number one.") The work of therapy, if the object of the threat is present in your client's life, will focus on changing the sickest relationship by measures such as these:

1. Identify anger as the source of the suicidal impulse.
2. Explore the threatener's current feelings toward the target.
3. Find out what the threatener would accept as amends if offered by the target.

The general theme of this kind of intervention is to normalize the threatener's feelings by suggesting that they are understandable and can be a subject of discussion.

In the therapy conversation, the client must acknowledge his or her anger, describe exactly what provoked it, and accept the premise that sacrificing a life to punish another is absurd. Further, if it is possible to bring the target into at least one session, a confrontation between protagonist and antagonist should prove beneficial. The purpose of this meeting will be to extract a face-to-face apology from the target. If it occurs, the client must decide whether or not it was genuine. If perceived as genuine, the apology must be followed by forgiveness on the part of the threatener. If forgiven, the target must promise never to do again what had been done. (This process is elaborated in Everstine and Everstine, 2006.). See figure 1.

When the threatener's antagonist is not available (dead, living far away, refusing to come in, etc.), the therapist's best strategy is to revise the client's history. For example, a person who was molested in childhood should find out, one way or another, what has become of the molester––punished, or if not punished, why not. The client should be encouraged to focus on what happened, the person who did it, and what was done about it. If nothing has been done, and if the statute of limitations has not expired, a criminal case can be opened. Whether or not charges are brought, the victim can consider filing a lawsuit against the molester. This kind of retaliation succeeds virtually as well in the conception as in the implementation. A suit may fail or have been filed too late, but the saving grace is the desire for retribution and the effort to make it happen. The cathartic part is to destroy the legacy of the perpetrator in the eyes of anyone who knew him.

There is more than one way to shield your client from harm––bureaucratic or self-inflicted. While the client comes to you for help in solving a problem or problems, he or she expects the consulting room to be a safe place, *sanctum sanctorum*. Keeping your client alive is the quintessential protection.

Another menace from which a client may potentially need protection is the therapist himself or herself. The staggering irony of this state of affairs has its origin in the famous Tarasoff case (1974, 1976). A complete account of this case and its implications for therapy is presented in Chapter 10, "Tarasoff Revisited."

6. AFFIRMING

Affirmation is the kindest gift that a therapist can give to a client. It serves to strengthen the client's ego, which is the healthiest element of a well-adjusted person, and similarly the most vulnerable. A sense of self is the first line of defense when life plays tricks, and the first to suffer when life overwhelms. The skills of establishing rapport, listening, remembering, protecting, and finding out converge in the intervention of affirming, the success of which will be the culmination of theirs.

The need for repair of the ego is strikingly clear when the person attempts to survive a traumatic event in which the threat to the person's identity leads to questions such as "Why me?" And later to questions like "Who am I now?" And for that matter, "Who was I before this terrible thing happened?"

Many people believe, at least subconsciously, that they have been major contributors to their woes, and assign blame to themselves without logical examination. In Freud's formula, this happens when the superego dominates the already poorly defended ego. In the interactional view that forms the theoretical orientation of this book, the internal process described by Freud is replaced by a focus on *external* causes of behavior. People are influenced in what they do, and in varying degrees are controlled by the behavior of others. This view has been applied to explain how people learn (Everstine, 2011), as well as causal factors in suicide (Everstine, 1998).

When a client launches into an account of his or her faults—"I should have finished college," "I ruined my marriage," "I can't concentrate at work," "I have no friends," "My wife's [husband's] family hates me"—the interactional approach to therapy means finding out what other person is the central figure in the client's dilemma. For example, "Who tells you that you should have finished college?" "Who is distracting you from your work?" "Why is your spouse rejecting you?" "What friend have you lost?" "Who in your wife's family dislikes you?" Probes of this kind rest on the premise that the client's troubles have arisen in a damaged or dysfunctional relationship with at least one other person. Once the key relationship(s) has (have) been identified, the client's therapy can begin. It consists of healing relationships.

Changing a person's perception of his or her troubles to an examination of the dyad in which the cause of the troubles lies redefines the attendant self-blame and lessens the assault on the beleaguered ego. This fundamental intervention is the first step toward affirmation.

Because a person's problems originate and are maintained in an interpersonal context, therapy treats the relationship. This process involves drawing out the facts of a series of interactions between the people, interpreting each event in terms of its effect on the client. From one point of view, this process resembles couple's counseling, except that it is not necessary (and often impossible) for the other member of the relationship to be present in the therapy sessions. While their interactions are the operative subject of interpretation, if rapport has been gained with the client, the nature of the relationship can be examined solely from the client's description of what occurs when the dyad interacts.

A person needs affirmation because he or she has been devalued in one or more aspect of the self by some other person. This rejection may not be consciously perceived, but it persists and spreads across the psyche like a slowly growing tumor. Far more debilitating than mere low self-esteem, the need for affirmation blocks or frustrates the simplest personal endeavors. The person fails inadvertently, or fails deliberately in a form of self-fulfilling prophesy, and ultimately embraces failure as though it were an inborn trait: he or she can do nothing right.

The first task of the therapist in helping a client who lacks affirmation is to identify the source of the disconfirming relationship or relationships in his or her life. An analogy would be trying to find the source of identity theft by tracing the record of breaches of computer security. Often the difficulty lies in quite obvious sectors of the person's current situation. Indeed, the antagonist may be a spouse, a former spouse, one or more family members, a boss, a coworker, or anyone who has broken the client's trust.

Whether intentionally or otherwise, the antagonist has wounded the protagonist's ego, which may have been vulnerable already. The person has wandered into a toxic relationship and has sought your advice on how to make it better.

Affirming is a process that entails increasing a client's sense of self by whatever means possible and to an unlimited degree; put simply, it is strengthening the ego. A therapist has a virtual license to employ any therapeutic technique, including deception. As subtly as possible, the therapist compliments the client's best qualities and ignores the flaws. In essence, the client has done nothing wrong and is not the only source of his or her problems. His or her relationships may be troubled, but the client must be considered no more than 50 percent accountable, with blame assigned to others proportionately.

Affirming involves the application of a purely secular ethic. For example, in the case of a man who has abandoned his wife and children for another woman, it is not within the role of the therapist to deplore his conduct but to help explain it, to place it in the proper context of the person's history and current psychological functioning. If he seeks moral condemnation, he will not get it in therapy. If he tries to make amends to his victims for what he did or to gain confidence that he will not do anything like it in the future, therapy can help. Because each of us, as a person, has a moral compass, being nonjudgmental may be the hardest of our tasks as caregivers. We should leave our righteous indignation outside the consulting room.

The major themes of affirming are variants of these:

1. Life has not treated you kindly.
2. You are a good person.
3. You have a tendency to doubt yourself.
4. What is happening to you is not only your fault.
5. Some of your relationships are not what they should be.
6. You owe it to yourself to improve these relationships or find new ones.
7. You must concentrate on the best qualities of your personality and bring them to the fore.

There is nothing grandiose about any of these steps to actualization. They are exercises for the impoverished ego; the accomplished therapist will reward them when expressed spontaneously, or attempt to elicit them when they are not forthcoming. The best affirmations are naturally those that originate in the client's new self-image.

Affirming is not fulsome praise. The therapist takes the client as given with a mosaic of unfulfilled promises and all too human foibles, and tries to find the best part of anything that he or she does or says. When in a therapy session, he or she is the center of attention, the focus of events, the one who sets the agenda. The purpose of this process is for the client to feel better about himself or herself.

7. LETTING GO

Good therapy is brief therapy. Although Freud's preferred model of treatment involved five sessions a week, for years in some instances, he was able to confront squarely the issue of case duration. His essay, "Analysis Terminable and Interminable," was published just two years before his death, one year before his exodus from Vienna to London. The essay serves as a summing up of Freud's thoughts about what the analytic movement had accomplished until then, as well as what he felt had been left undone. This valediction concluded:

> It is not my intention to assert that analysis in general is an endless business . . . I believe that in practice analyses do come to an end . . . The business of analysis is to secure the best psychological conditions for the functioning of the ego; when this has been done, analysis has accomplished its task.

Of course, the decision on whether or not the conditions had been "secured" was one that he reserved for himself. We cannot forget that Freud never worked for insurance companies, nor did he charge on a sliding scale. To prolong therapy, he had both motive and opportunity.

In practical terms, there is little justification for keeping a client in therapy until he or she can no longer afford it, or until the quota of visits set by the insurance company has been reached. Instead, the task of the therapist is to provide the best care possible in as few visits as possible. No one should be persuaded to spend fifty minutes in a consulting room once a week indefinitely.

A therapist owes it to the client to observe carefully when the therapy goals, stated or unstated, have been met. Freud noted that when his client was late in coming to an appointment or did not appear at all, the client was sending a subtle message that treatment should soon end. While this was merely Freud's intuition, it contains a grain of truth.

Because the client is the best judge of how long therapy should continue, it is wise to try and discover how he or she feels about the subject. This attempt requires considerable subtlety and judicious timing. A client should not be given the impression that the therapist has tired of their meetings. Even so, it is in the best interest of the client to be released from therapy as soon as its benefits have been maximized. A wise approach on the part of the therapist is to broach the subject and defer to the client's wishes. "You seem to be doing well lately. Do you prefer to make our next meeting on an as-needed basis? You can call me anytime and we can talk on the phone or get together soon." A good observer will watch the client's reaction to this suggestion, noting the nonverbal behavior, including the inflection of the voice in his or her reply. If the reaction has the slightest negative connotation, the subject should be dropped and replaced by a different line of questioning. Your client isn't ready.

Often, when the offer to end therapy is made and rejected, the client may bring an entirely new problem to be solved. Sometimes an historical narrative that was related only in passing will be revisited, embellished with crucial details that were suppressed because they were too revealing or too disturbing to tell. The client who chooses not to end treatment sees this as a last chance to get to the heart of the matter. A new chapter in therapy begins.

A breakthrough like this can occur when a client, who previously said something like "I had a lousy childhood," will return to the subject by saying that he or she was a victim of child abuse, and the full story of that experience and its aftermath will tumble out as if a locked door had been opened. From the client's point of view, he or she may have thought that the therapist had intuited this earlier in treatment. The relief when it is revealed will be enhanced by the pride of having broken silence voluntarily. For a therapist, moments such as these are true epiphanies. The course of treatment is rejuvenated and can start again on the right track, mining a new vein of disclosure and healing. Trust is reaffirmed and the transference remains intact.

Even so, problems emerging just when therapy was about to end do not justify prolonging therapy indefinitely. The therapist must consider that a too well established counter-transference may be at work. Perhaps the client is seen as a "nice person" whose cooperation in therapy flatters the clinician, or whose conversation on general topics is pleasing. Or it may be that the client "invents" one difficulty after another to continue the relationship. Others have described this phenomenon in its extreme form as "the purchase of friendship." It is well within the proper role of a therapist to limit this form of pathology by controlling the process of saying goodbye. We should recognize when it is time to get out of the way and wish the client well. Life is not therapy, nor is therapy life.

It is scarcely ethical and certainly rude to contact a client when it has been made clear that therapy has ended. Calling to ask "How are you doing?" is transparently selfish because it begs for compliments. If it was established at the last session that the client is welcome to call the therapist at any time when needed, there is good reason for not *initiating* contact.

II. PERSPECTIVES

8. COUPLES AT WAR

Those who have worked with couples are well aware that couple's therapy is qualitatively different from individual work. With one person, the focus is on changing personality dynamics; with a couple, it is a relationship that you seek to change. The complexities of sorting out the problems of two people as opposed to one are not merely additive. The therapist enters a maelstrom of conflict between the two partners that has probably begun long ago. What has brought them to therapy is a fervent wish to find peace in their relationship. And just as the attraction of person A to person B is often greater than the attraction of person B to A, there is likely more motivation for counseling on the part of one as opposed to the other. This lack of synchronicity may be symptomatic of the conflict itself, and the lack of commitment of one person to therapy will impede therapy if not repaired.[1]

Balancing the commitments of the two participants relies on the establishment of rapport with both. And because no therapy can be successful unless some measure of rapport has occurred, if one member of the couple misses sessions or avoids participation in the sessions the best strategy may be to recommend individual treatment for each, at least temporarily. Of course, many therapists who work with couples prefer to have a session with A alone, followed by a session with B, with joint sessions interspersed. The only caveat against such an arrangement is that it may prolong the course of therapy needlessly. The most effective work of couple's therapy occurs when both partners are working on confronting their issues face to face with a mediator present. The only advantages to be gained from separate sessions would be to promote self-reflection and a cooling of emotions stirred up by confrontation.

What presenting problem most often motivates a couple for counseling? In their words, it is often some version of "We can't communicate." Just as often, I doubt the accuracy of this characterization of the difficulty between them. But if I observe them and one partner repeatedly interrupts what the other is saying or "talks over" the other, there is no denying that a communication problem exists. It will be vital to deal with this immediately in therapy by saying something like, "I have a hard and fast rule for these sessions, and that is only one speaks at a time." Once introduced, this rule must be strictly enforced.

More prevalent than this scenario is one in which the partners communicate *all too well*. After the "no interruption" rule is established, it often becomes clear that the difficulty lies not in the form but the content of their communication: they do not share the same values. Values are deeply held views of what is important in life, what is worth doing, what kind of person is "good," etc. These judgments are taught within the first few years of life by those who play parental roles. (According to one study, they are ingrained by the seventh year.) Beliefs like these, so molded into the person's character, may last a lifetime. If altered, it is probably a result of the person's reaching a milestone such as a threatening illness, death of a friend or close relative, the empty nest, serious accident, fiftieth birthday, etc. Intimations of mortality such as these is sufficient to cause one to reassess any long-held belief.

When partners in a marriage clash about values, the fact of the matter may be too daunting to discuss. After all, if a value is as programmed as the color of one's hair, change is problematic at best. Each person might feel helpless to influence the other person's point of view. That's how a value judgment can become a taboo subject. A mother will complain that the children's father is too indulgent with them. A husband will attribute poor money management to his wife. Both will disagree about the importance of religion in their lives, and one will accuse the other of being too committed to religious participation. One seeks social stimulation, while the other is content to stay at home.

When it comes to choosing a life partner, we must accept that sometimes Providence is a poor matchmaker. Everyone knows that our choices depend heavily on luck, but we tend to forget that hazard when infatuated. There is no scale on which the values of each person can be weighed against the other to see if they are comparable. Too much is left to chance, but that is a source of much of the adventure of relationship. After all, our life stories often amount to learning to play the hand we have been dealt.

Early in counseling it may become clear that your couple is engaged in a power struggle. If so, the first step is to determine to what extent the relationship is impaired by this conflict. At some point the couple should be told that the struggle is transparent to the therapist, and they should show some willingness to acknowledge it. What has happened is that the partners have not decided who is to dominate the relationship, or who is to exert the most influence over the other. The balance of power may have changed over time, but the therapist must measure it as it is now and seek to right the ship.

An intense, protracted power struggle between partners can have one of two outcomes: compromise or temporary separation. To prevent the necessity of the latter, it may be wise to propose a "time-out" when the combatants move away from each other either outside the house, inside the house, or symbolically for a short while. This space should permit a cooling of emotions as well as mature reflection on (a) the state of the relationship (b) the intensity of mutual anger (c) the utility of being together as opposed to being apart, and (d) the terms of apology required by each side. Depending on their preference, therapy can be done in independent sessions during the separation, or they can make their only meetings couple's sessions. The therapist should monitor their progress while apart, and encourage reconciliation as soon as possible.

The source of the couple's conflict will be found in the minutiae of their *disagreements*. However petty and superfluous they may seem, these clashes and disconnects hold the motives on which this war is based. The task of the therapist is to untangle the crossed and knotted threads that lie at the heart of their bond. Picking them apart is not easy and requires sufficient rapport with the couple to permit them to describe their quarrels in full detail. Once they trust you, it will be "he said, she said" from then on.

Some spouses are masters of the art of the quarrel. The stronger the relationship, the more likely these stages will be reached, in sequence.

STAGES OF THE QUARREL

Oppositional: "We simply don't agree."

Adversarial: "You don't understand what I am saying."

Accusatory: "You have a closed mind."

Inflammatory: "You only think of yourself."

Incendiary: "You make me sick."

Hurtful: "I hate you."

Intimidating: "You can be replaced."

When the antagonists reach this last, climactic stage, the battle has been joined. Peace can be attained and equilibrium restored when these stages of peacemaking have been reached.

STAGES OF RECOVERY

Collaboration: "The dog has to be taken to the vet."
Reminiscing: "We were so happy then."
Reflection: "You have had a bad day."
Concession: "What I said must have hurt."
Apology: "I'm sorry."
Olive branch: "Let's talk."
Peace offering: "Can we go out for dinner tomorrow?"

Leading the adversaries through these stages to recovery is not a simple matter; often the stages are interchanged, and in many cases excruciatingly slow in coming. Even so, a couple that can survive a major quarrel is much the better for it. In short, peacemaking between dueling partners is the truest test of the couple's counselor's art.

When jealousy, which has destroyed more relationships than infidelity itself, is revealed in the course of therapy, it must be dealt with quickly and decisively. This emotion serves no purpose in human life, having been spawned by the Devil to wreak havoc on relationships. At the core of jealousy is fear, and the fear arises from a deep-seated lack of self-esteem. These dynamics should be explained to the partners, preferably in separate sessions, so that each can get a perspective on this pathetic weakness. The jealous person should learn that what he or she is feeling is not so much betrayal as a sense of inadequacy, and begin to confront how dependent he or she has become. The accused partner, whether guilty of infidelity or not, should accept that the accuser is not malicious but is expressing a fear of abandonment that began long ago, probably before they ever met. In any case, jealous feelings and accusations are anathema to couple's therapy.

Most therapists agree that if a client admits to being in an affair while couple's therapy is in progress, therapy should be suspended until there is evidence that the affair has ended. In fact, most clients will accept this rule amiably because both partners admit that the situation is patently counterproductive to improvement in a relationship.

Working with a couple to help them appreciate each other more is well worth doing because of the considerable investment that each has made in the relationship. In nine out of ten couples, there were tender feelings, perhaps genuine love for each other, at some time in their history together. This is the basis for success in therapy, and it behooves the therapist to build his or her interventions on this bond.

9. CASES IN POINT

The paradox of the case histories that are found in many therapy manuals is that the story must be altered to protect client privacy. The criterion is that a client, should he or she read the case history, would disavow most of the details, and an acquaintance of the client would not know who it was. The result is that case histories are necessarily fictionalized accounts that are intended more to instruct than to record. In the following, several cases in the writer's experience have been co-mingled.

THEIR BROTHER'S KEEPERS

Searching for the vortex of a troubled psyche may take you to the distant past, even the dimly remembered recent past. A man suffers from a sense of worthlessness in midlife, a lack of purpose, a want of pride, a feeling of having "accomplished nothing" in his life and of lacking a compass to guide his future. On the surface he is the Hollow Man, having been nowhere and having nowhere to go. He finds this malaise baffling. Nothing at the surface of his life is oppressive——not his boss, his wife, or his children; indeed, his wife is abundantly supportive. Who is he? What went wrong? Where is the enemy? What should he do to free himself from this quicksand that threatens to swallow life?

If this is a familiar story for therapists, their approach might follow guidelines such as these.

1. The person's past must be thoroughly explored.
2. At least one person in the client's past will have been responsible for this illness.
3. The responsible person(s) will not have accepted responsibility for what was done to the client, therefore will not have been punished for it.

The specific circumstances of what happened to plant the seeds of the client's current symptoms are irrelevant here. Nevertheless, it is important that the client identify the "guilty" party and acknowledge that he or she has "unfinished business" with that person.

In our hero's case, many probing questions revealed that beginning in early adolescence and continuing in one form or another until his current middle age, he had been bullied by two older brothers. Even as adults, their mother's death and the division of her estate brought forth a firestorm of domineering behavior on the part of the brothers. Truly, from childhood until

THE ART OF THERAPY

recently, the client had unfinished business with them. The client has tried to be cordial with them, at least to avoid a fight, and the three men have settled into an unholy alliance to bury the past. The older brothers have no sympathy for the client's chronic depression, and the latter's efforts to placate them continue. The goal of therapy is to heal those ancient wounds, and it will require the active participation of the client himself. As a foretaste of what is to come, empty chair exercises can be a useful first step.

Empty chair as a form of rehearsal for the face-to-face confrontation that will later take place can focus on themes such as these.

1. If your older brother [middle brother] was sitting in that chair and you could say anything you wished, what would you say to him?
2. If your parents were watching you as you spoke to your brother, how would that affect what you might say?
3. When confronted with what you were saying, how would your older brother [middle brother] react? What would he reply?

Questions such as these are neutral, with no particular emotions implied, but they would only be a prelude to what would be said in a face-to-face interaction. For example:

"When we were young, I thought that you bullied me. Did you?"

"When our mother died, I thought that you pushed me out of the process of caring for her estate. How did you feel about that?"

And of course, the ultimate questions:

"Are you sorry for the way you treated me as a child?"

"Are you sorry for the way you treated me when mother died?"

An actual confrontation such as the one scripted above may be risky but may advance therapy in ways that could only be achieved in many discursive sessions. The role of the therapist is to mediate the interchange and present emotions from getting out of hand.

To the extent that this process, taken seriously by both parties, can ultimately have a peaceful resolution, these events are crucial.

1. An apology will be made by the antagonist
2. The protagonist will consider the apology to be genuine
3. The protagonist will forgive the other person
4. The oppressor will promise the oppressed person not to do anything of the kind again

PREVENTING SUICIDE[1]

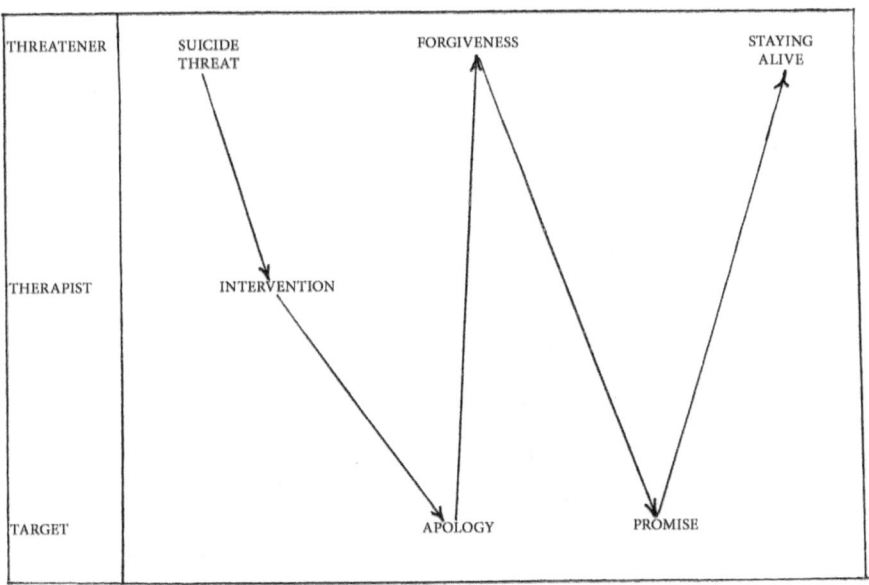

1. Adapted from a diagram used to illustrate the process of suicide prevention (Everstine, 2004).

The role of the therapist is to facilitate this process, moving it along if it gets stuck in one phase or another. Of course, in many cases this sequence occurs naturally, without benefit of therapy.

The three brothers of this example may never resolve their tangled conflict; perhaps one or the other lacks the capacity for real change. At least, our client will know where the trouble lies, will be alert when one of his brothers goes back on his promise, and may be able to forgive himself for his original passivity toward them.

NO WAY OUT

A woman in her fifties came to see me because I had counseled her son years before. She felt that she was depressed and dreaded the coming visit to family for Christmas because she had been told that her brother would be there—a rare visit. She confided that when they were teenagers this older brother had molested her repeatedly for many years, and without her parents' knowing. Of course, she had been afraid to tell them because it would break their hearts and lead to unceasing family strife.

Somehow the molestation was discovered and ended by her parents' intervention. A criminal charge was brought against the boy, still a juvenile; and when a hearing was conducted, she was kept out of the courtroom. Her grandfather became a witness on behalf of her brother, and the result of the hearing was that the charges against her brother were dropped and the case closed. She was not even given a transcript of the hearing. The client never forgave the grandfather, who died before she came to me. How she felt about his betrayal was never expressed to him.

At later sessions she said that she had decided not to confront her brother at the Christmas meeting. Instead, she was trying to find out how to get a copy of the hearing transcript from the court. Clearly she was motivated to learn what she could about both her brother and grandfather, without knowing what she would do when she found out. This business was not finished.

There the story of her therapy ends. Christmas came and went without a word from her, and one can only guess whether she was able to wrest an apology from one or both of her parents for not protecting her from abuse, nor whether she was able to find out what had happened in the criminal case. At best, she may have been able to join her brother in some form of truce.

The television talk show host Dick Cavett would pause after interviewing a guest at length and ask the question, "What can we learn from this?" What can we learn from this case of family cruelty?

Childhood abuse, especially sexual abuse, leaves indelible scars. Memories of what it was like will go with the victim to his or her grave. (A therapist can expect no more than an abridged account.) But even repression of profound traumatic events has a shelf life of its own. For example, anniversaries of events such as these can trigger intense but inexplicable anxious feelings as though something must emerge from memory but can't.

The memories of a victim of intra-family child sexual abuse are pathologized by feelings such as these:

1. Those who should have protected me have failed me.
2. My assailant has not been sufficiently punished for what was done to me.
3. Some may feel that I bear complicity for what happened, such as that I was a willing participant in what took place.
4. Even if he was to be punished, I would not be healed and my memories would torture me *ad infinitum*.
5. My virginity was stolen from me.

6. Anyone who loves me must be told of this stain on my virtue.

7. My parents preferred the molester to me.

8. Everyone will know about this, or think they know, and make up stories about me.

Some cases leave their victim with resentment toward the justice system for not punishing the assailant sufficiently. Thoughts such as these will occur without warning, obtrusively, for as long as the trauma is unresolved. They will spawn a lifetime of conflicts and confusion and inexplicable symptoms both mental and physical. This is the legacy of a child sexual abuse that has not been laid to rest.

STURM UND DRANG

Paul, seventeen, is one mixed-up kid. I first saw him in therapy when he was fourteen. He was essentially a normal teenager whose problems were more or less evenly divided among school, home life, and friends. His parents were often in conflict, threatening each other with divorce. His grades were just good enough to enable him to be promoted. His four or five best friends did a lot of "hanging out" at a local park, but he had no formal girlfriend. We talked about each of his encounters with potential girlfriends, weighing the strengths and weaknesses of each relationship. We talked about the anxiety in his household that was created by the parents' chronic quarrels. We discussed the possibility of his changing from one high school to another to find more compatible friends and more sympathetic teachers.

Less than a year later, Paul's life underwent a sea change. He fell in love with an Internet friend, Samantha, about the same age. She lived with her family some three thousand miles away. Paul's infatuation with her grew stronger by the day. They exchanged photographs, life stories, and fantasies about their futures. Their interactions progressed from daily cell phone calls to calls plus e-mails, to calls plus e-mails plus text messages. His parents, appalled by this apparently futile romance, took away his cell phone and monitored his use of the family phone and his computer. Paul rebelled angrily at this oppressive control, but when his behavior became more and more placating, they gave him permission to get in touch with her again.

So continued the cyberspace courtship, as well as the joust with the parents. The star-crossed lovers began to speculate about meeting in person and lobbied the parents of each to entertain the idea. Samantha, a home-schooled student, could travel most anytime, but no matter who made the journey it would be a financial hardship. For his part, Paul insisted stridently that his parents take the relationship seriously, throwing tantrums, barricading himself in his room, punching walls, and generally behaving like a wild person. The parents were so upset at this development that they announced that they would take Paul to the other city to meet Samantha in person.

The visit occurred without incident. Paul and his parents returned home, and the long-distance courtship resumed apace.

Having met the girl of his dreams in person, Paul was even more smitten than before. Their meeting had gone smoothly, and they had established some reason to believe that they would be compatible.

Time had not treated Samantha and Paul well. His family welcomed her to their home on one occasion, accompanied by her brother, and the two families blended well enough. Then there were more months of separation. Finally, Paul was calling and texting her in the middle of the night so often that his parents confiscated his phone. This offended him so deeply that his rages intensified, leading to more destruction of his room. Twice the father called the police in exasperation, and on each occasion Paul was carted off to the local mental health ward, where he was kept for three days and discharged by the staff in its bafflement about him. One time, he was prescribed Seroquel because the staff could not fathom his bizarre ramblings.

In therapy with Paul, which began long before he discovered Samantha, our conversations were grounded in teenaged versions of Freud's *lieben und arbeiten* (love and work). We had talked about his ever-changing peer group, discussed romance, his struggles with high school and then home school, his thoughts about a career, and his random musings about life and the world. In short, the natural content of supportive therapy.

I got frequent calls from Paul's parents, usually telling me about his latest episode of lunacy. Of course, instead of telling them that I shouldn't be discussing Paul in detail because of his confidentiality rights, I listened without comment and gave a mini lecture on the mysteries of adolescence.

What is happening in the teenage years is what the psychiatrist Carl Whitaker called a time of "malignant isolation." The child begins to realize that childhood is over. The task before him is to prepare himself for life apart from parental control. To do that, he must question each attempt to control him and defy it if possible. He is establishing his ego, his sense of self, his personhood. For many young people, this process is an excruciating struggle, as distressing as, one speculates, the butterfly's emergence from the chrysalis. Most parents look upon this process with astonishment bordering on horror. Their basic belief is that the adolescent could not possibly survive on his own. Their need to protect him clouds their perception of what it would be like to let him go. The struggle begins.

Paul's parents have trouble seeing that the best way to help in his misery is to accept it and try to contain it, but in essence let it happen. Frank recall of their own transitions can give them perspective. The relationship between Samantha and Paul is likely to wither, especially when either one or both enters young adulthood. For now the grownups should reflect on the lesson given by Shakespeare in *Romeo and Juliet*, trying to keep people from loving each other is a futile aim. In the play, the two families' attempts to separate the lovers end with both of them lying dead on the stage. Never try to separate two people who love each other. It's a losing game.

10. TARASOFF REVISITED

Those who have the temerity to pursue a career in mental health are soon made aware of the multicultural taboo against mental illness, and by extension, those who derive a living from it. It is said that psychiatry, for example, has less prestige in the medical world than any other discipline save perhaps podiatry. (Reaction to this snub may have contributed to the collective decision of psychiatrists to abandon medicine in favor of pharmacology.)

Psychotherapists are a charitable lot, second only to nurses in their caring for the welfare of others. Psychotherapists are also inveterate rule followers who have never met a bureaucratic directive that they would not obey. Worse yet, their wages per hour are lower than the wages of their plumbers or car mechanics, and they haven't the will to protest. As an example of their passivity, therapists in California were recently required to have their fingerprints taken at their expense, and to see to it that their results were forwarded to the State Department of Justice. Big Brother watches over them as though they were potential criminals who could harm the populace and should be kept under surveillance. No one asked in advance if therapists wished to challenge this abuse of power or contest its premise.

Typical of the efforts to govern mental health care from a distance was the infamous Tarasoff case (referred to above, Chapter 3). The justices of the California Supreme Court, having no knowledge of or feeling for the therapy process, imposed a judgment in a lawsuit that sent ominous ripples far from California to our entire profession. For many therapists the events of this case may be dim in memory, and for the recent graduate, ancient history. Here is a full account.

In 1976, the California Supreme Court handed down a decision that affected the work of every therapist and the lives of every client of psychotherapy. The story began in 1969 in Berkeley, California. A student from India, Prosenjit Poddar, fell in love with Tatiana Tarasoff, also a college student. By all accounts, she soon spurned his attentions, leaving for a summer vacation in Brazil. Poddar entered therapy at the psychiatry clinic of the student health center, and told his psychologist, Dr. Lawrence Moore, that he was planning to kill a girl he knew. While he did not name the girl, it was later established that Dr. Moore had ample knowledge of who she was. Following this visit, Dr. Moore telephoned the campus police, asking that they detain Poddar for the purpose of taking him to a mental hospital for observation. A letter was sent to the chief of the campus police with the same request. Three officers took Poddar into custody, questioned him, decided that he was rational, and let him go with a warning to stay away from Tatiana.

The next scene of this drama took place in the office of the clinic director, Dr. Harvey Powelson. Powelson, a psychiatrist, asked the chief of police to return Dr. Moore's letter and had copies of the letter destroyed. Also destroyed were notes that Moore had made about his client. Finally, Powelson ordered no action be taken to place Prosenjit Poddar in a seventy-two-hour treatment and evaluation facility. Poddar never returned to therapy. He persuaded Tatiana's brother to share an apartment with him near her house. Shortly after she returned from Brazil, he went to the house, called her to the door, and stabbed her. She ran into the front yard, collapsed, and died. Poddar himself reported the killing to the police.

At his trial, Poddar claimed that he himself had warned his victim. He was convicted of second-degree murder and spent five years in jail, whereupon his conviction was overturned on appeal. An arrangement was made by which he would not be retried if he left the country. With this murderer's release from jail and his departure for India, the curtain fell on a Chekhovian tragedy.

While Poddar was in jail waiting for his appeal to be heard, the Tarasoff family filed suit against the university and, by extension, the State of California. Named in the suit were Dr. Moore, Dr. Powelson, two other psychiatrists of the clinic, and the campus police—all employees of the state. At the local level the suit was decided in favor of the defendants, meaning that Tatiana's family lost. The case was appealed to the California Supreme Court, where the final decision was rendered in 1976.

The Tarasoff suit had brought charges against the university for two acts of omission that contributed to Tatiana's death: (1) failing to hospitalize Poddar and (2) failing to warn her parents of the threat against her life. Suffice it to say that the first charge, failure to hospitalize, was brushed aside by the court because the defendants enjoyed *immunity* from being liable for not putting someone in hospital by virtue of their being state employees. In sum, the court did *not* take a position on the subject of hospitalizing a person who is dangerous to others.

When a case reaches the Supreme Court level, arguments can be put forward by groups or persons who have only indirect interest in the matter at hand. The justices who heard Tarasoff received several "friend of the court" briefs from the American Psychiatric Association and other therapist organizations. These briefs rounded up the usual disclaimers that spring to mind when therapists must look violence squarely in the face. For example, therapists (quoting now from the Psychiatric Association) "are unable reliably to predict violent acts." Other examples include the view that the privacy of the consulting room is sacred, and that breaches of confidentiality––such as the one advocated in Tarasoff––would deter troubled people from enrolling in psychotherapy in future. The Supreme Court cut a wide swath through each of these arguments. To the lament that a therapist cannot foresee violent acts, the justices noted that Dr. Moore had indeed predicted violence. His actions clearly showed that he perceived Poddar's threat as a real one, and the sad events that followed proved him to be a true prophet.

As far as the confidentiality privilege is concerned, the justices reminded the friends of the court that there are many exceptions to the privilege in both medicine and social services, such as when a physician must reveal that his or her patient has contracted a communicable disease, or when a health officer must quarantine people during an epidemic. And if the examining room of a medical doctor is not a secret place, why then should a therapist's office be? In fact, the very laws that protect confidentiality in most states have a host of exceptions requiring that a breach be made in certain circumstances. And that was amply true in California, where the following had been written into law four years before the Tarasoff murder, "There is no privilege . . . if the psychotherapist has reasonable cause to believe that the patient is in such mental or emotional condition as to be dangerous to himself or to the person or property of another, and that *disclosure of the communication* is necessary to prevent the threatened danger." This clause in the law was the basis of the court's decision, and its first judicial test was the Tarasoff case.

To the argument that potentially violent people would be deterred from entering therapy if a warning were required, the court believed it unlikely that a potentially violent person enters therapy expecting that his or her threats will be kept secret. Further, how would the therapist's silence make therapy more productive? From another perspective, even if a therapist made a promise at the outset of treatment never to reveal a word that was said, how would that promise help persuade a client to give up thoughts of violence? These questions the justices could not answer, nor could the friends of the court answer for them. As a result, the case was decided in favor of the plaintiffs, with the judicial conclusion that resounds like a cathedral bell: "The protective privilege ends where the public peril begins."

These were the final developments: the court decreed that the parents did have a valid reason for their suit and returned the case for possible trial. That never happened. The arguments on both sides were not debated in a public forum, and no admission of negligence was obtained from the university or its therapists. Instead, a settlement on a certain sum of money was negotiated, but the amount was never made public. In the ultimate irony, a blanket of privacy was drawn over this case that challenged the *right* to privacy.

Over the years, there have been strong reactions against the Tarasoff rule, to the extent that therapists have appealed to their state representatives for legislative relief. One such attempt occurred in California, where a bill was passed giving immunity for failure to warn if the threat was not a "serious" one. As far as the warning itself, this law required that a therapist make only "reasonable efforts." What these efforts might be was unstated, meaning that future test cases would define them. But the law had a disturbing final clause as expressed in these words, ". . . reasonable efforts to communicate the threat to the victim and to a law enforcement agency." The word "and" is the key here, because it goes far beyond Tarasoff in which warning *or* notifying the police would suffice.

This second requirement, very likely, is honored more in the breach than the observance. It's especially ludicrous for anyone who has called upon the police to intervene in a situation involving mental illness. The most likely outcome is either that the police will do nothing or will do the wrong thing. For instance, if a client requires hospitalization most of us will choose among many ways to accomplish that task without asking help from the police. It was Brendan Behan, the Irish poet and playwright, who wrote that "There is no situation of human misery that cannot be made worse by the presence of a policeman."

It would be hard to imagine a more crushing blow to the client confidentiality privilege than the duty to warn, and its requirement that therapists become police informants. Worse, subsequent litigation has "strengthened" the duty to warn mandate to the extent that in California there are now at least eighteen exceptions to the privilege. Worse yet, the duty has been stretched out of shape to the extent of being a "duty to protect," namely to *prevent* the warned person from being harmed.

Many police agencies have adopted the motto "to protect and serve." Apparently therapists are being deputized to aid police in preventing violence. This role is light-years beyond those that a therapist normally expects when leaving graduate school, such as being a caring "parent," sympathetic "uncle," concerned "sibling," or a helpful "friend." We are often called upon to be "our brother's keeper," but that does not imply being his bodyguard.[1]

One omission found in the Tarasoff decision, later corrected by critics of the decision (see Everstine, et al., 1980) is that the duty to warn implies a duty to warn of the duty to warn. Recognition of this logic has led to a universal resolve among therapists to provide a statement to the client before therapy begins, explaining these constraints upon total confidentiality. In the statement, the therapist's duties to warn, "protect," and inform the police are spelled out, and the client is asked to accept by signature. Naturally, this pact is itself a threat to the fundamental building block of therapy, rapport.

Does this mean that the Tarasoff requirement, stupid as it was, has dealt a death blow to client confidentiality? No, it hasn't, but it has certainly made it unlikely that anyone who intends to harm another person will mention it in therapy. Because it was not thought through, the attempt of the court to enroll therapists in the "stamp out violence" brigade has fallen of its own weight. Therapists obviously deplore violence, but their basic role has never been, or will be, to act as informers of the police or as security officers for people they've never met.

11. PLOYS

For the most part, therapy is an intuitive process, from the therapist's thoughts to the applied intervention. Even so, there are moments along the way when a new perspective must be supplied to the client, changing the flow of the dialogues in a radical way. As with any conversation, there are highs and lows in the course of a therapy session, and the therapist must be attentive to client boredom and respond to it.

Some questions that can be used to dispel the client's malaise include these:

> What do you plan to be doing and where will you be living five years from now? (Supply the date for emphasis.)

> What was the one event in your life that had the

most impact on you, the way you think, or the way
you live?

Who was the most influential person in your life
until now? How did you meet?

Answers to questions such as these, augmented by answers to
the Sentence Completion Test (Chapter 3), can yield fresh insights
into personality dynamics.

One way to challenge the client to "think outside the box" is
to invoke a fantasy authority who can make what, if the therapist
made it, would seem an outrageous suggestion for change. For
example, if the client suffers from an oppressive job situation, you
can say, "What if the judge issued an order requiring you to resign
from your job next Monday?"

There is no judge nor is there an order, but the client can be
reminded that "if you disobey a judge's order, you can be sent to
jail." Immediately the client will give you an indication (verbally or
nonverbally) of how much he or she is dependent on the job; in this
way you will directly engage the person's value system in which he
or she has accepted certain obligations. For example, remain loyal
to the employer, keep the job on behalf of a spouse or the family
or a parent who has admonished "never be a quitter." The client's
implicit fear of finding a new job or the lack of this fear will soon
come to the fore and be a rough measure of ego strength.

The same tactic can be used to ferret out feelings about various
situations and events. For example,

What if a judge issued an order that you must call your father, with whom you have not spoken in ten years, before the end of the month?

What if the judge issued an order that you will find an excuse not to attend the family's Thanksgiving dinner because it was so emotionally distressing last year?

Some ploys are more intrusive and require sensitive presentation as no more than hypotheses. One can say, "I'm going to give you a hypothetical." Caution such as this applies to questions such as these, "You say that you hate your brother. What if he were walking along the street and a brick fell on his head and he would no longer be with us, would you go to his funeral?" If yes, "Would you cry?" "The day after the funeral, what would you do that you hadn't done before that day?"

The same probe can be tried with, for example, a client who was molested as a child and now in adulthood harbors an unexpressed hatred toward the molester. "If the molester died today, would you go to the funeral?" A question of this kind is akin to the situation when a dentist's drill touches a nerve. An apology must be offered if the question probes too deeply.

Other questions seek more intimate feelings and must be asked with extreme sensitivity. E.g., "What if your husband (wife, lover) left you today?" In a variation on the traditional "empty chair" tactic, the therapist can point to an unoccupied chair and ask, for example in the case of a clash between mother and son, "If I brought your mother here and she was sitting in that chair, what would she say if I asked her 'What's wrong with this boy?'" In a marital conflict, you could ask one spouse, say a wife, "If your husband were here and I asked him what's wrong with his wife, what would he say?" Questions of this sort are generally unexpected, and true answers rely on the privacy of the consulting room, as well as the spoken or implicit pledge of the therapist not to "tell tales out of school"; i.e., to keep what was said confidential. Often the response of the person being asked the question is startling, and offers a sharp focus on the nature of the relationship.

Far more than manipulation, ploys such as these can puncture the dialogue with new perspectives, and yield quick, unvarnished revelations of a client's true feelings about a relationship that might otherwise have been concealed during hours of conventional interviewing. Here is information that even the keenest intuition might not have discovered.

Normally probes such as these will not cause the client discomfort or embarrassment if wielded gently. If the person shows a negative reaction to a question, one can say, "I didn't mean to put you on the spot." If indicated, withdraw the question and say you are sorry for asking it.

12. VALUES

Psychologists have determined that basic human values—what is good or bad, right or wrong, what is worth doing in life—are inculcated in the child by the age of nine. By adulthood, these principles of conduct are, for most people, deeply embedded in the subconscious. Suffice it to say that they are vigorously defended when challenged.

This subject, which is not taught in graduate schools nor occurs to the members of licensing boards, will be discussed here; namely, therapist values and the role they play for both therapist and client in the therapy experience. There would be no reason to expect that the partners in this relationship would share the same value system. Perspective on this potentially complicating factor is worth seeking.

We often come face to face with the values of our clients. A client might ask, "Do you believe in God?" Another might advocate a favored form of child discipline that to you is unacceptably harsh. Another might make a comment about immigrants that you would see as mean-spirited. We weather these detours in the course of therapy because they reveal details of the person's inner life that we might otherwise not have known. And for the sake of the relationship, we do our best not to be judgmental.

In service of the therapeutic relationship, it may be useful for a clinician to examine his or her own personal values as a precaution against bias. Ask yourself what are your true feelings on subjects like these:

> making money
> abortion
> capital punishment
> the role of religion in life
> obligations to elders
> euthanasia
> school grades based primarily on homework or on test scores
> political belief
> war and peace
> care of animals
> living to work or working to live

Each topic of this sort is thought about or talked about by each of us frequently, and we have formed positions on each. Our clients need not know these positions, but we must acknowledge them to ourselves and strive to keep them hidden when we are in the consulting room. For example, advising a client to pray more often would be an error of judgment. In therapy every therapist is an agnostic. Moral guidance is not part of your task. You have no mandate to point out to your client what is right or wrong in ethics. Naturally if he or she threatens to harm someone, you are indeed empowered to act decisively to prevent it from happening, assuming that the client has been warned in advance that you are obliged to do so. Further, try not to judge your client relying on the biblical injunction "leave her [him] to heaven"; i.e., let a higher authority be the judge.

For the client, each issue that he or she brings forth in therapy is critical and requires urgent attention. Some possible scenarios are identified in the following list of common presenting problems, posing for the clinician questions such as these.

What do you say when:

Your client learns that he or she has a terminal illness

A wife wants to carry her unborn child to term, but the husband prefers an abortion

Your client cannot decide whether or not to approve the euthanasia of her mother, who suffers from the last stages of Alzheimer's

One partner wants to draw the other into a religious group whose values the other cannot accept

Your client's adolescent child has just revealed that he or she is gay

Your client announces that he or she is planning to propose marriage to a person of another race

Your client feels that his or her partner's family is interfering in their relationship

A client is threatened with divorce because of an inability to manage the couple's money properly

Your client has proposed marriage to a partner, but the partner is afraid of commitment

These value-laden issues are not by themselves good or bad; there are no correct answers to the dilemmas they pose. What is important is that a therapist identify, acknowledge, and accept his or her immediate gut reactions to them as they arise, and assess how rigidly held his or her feelings are about them. If for example you oppose abortion on principle, your advice to a couple that is debating the means to solve a problem must be value-free. Try to avoid taking a position on the matter. The mere fact that the subject has arisen in therapy is testament to the rapport that you established early on. Your silence on the point will remind them that sooner or later their choices in value-laden decisions such as these will be theirs alone, and a tribute to the independence they will enjoy when a therapist is no longer around. Here, after all, is the goal for which therapy strives.

NOTES

INTRODUCTION

1.

The seven chapters included in this section, "Primary Colors," use individual counseling as the model being discussed. Couple's counseling is the subject of Chapter 8.

2.

One doesn't have to have been divorced to help a person who is facing divorce, but it would be useful to have observed more than one divorce with a discerning eye.

3.

For actual case examples of harm done by therapies such as these, see Singer and Lolich (1996).

ESTABLISHING RAPPORT

1.

Jones, E. (1953, p. 242)

2.

Ibid.

3.

Throughout, "client" will be used for more than one client when appropriate.

4.

The author is licensed to practice in California, and therefore is currently informed about only the ethical standards and confidentiality laws of that state.

LISTENING

1.

Everstine and Everstine (1993)

2.

In rich irony, because psychiatrists have chosen not to do therapy and only prescribe drugs, they no longer have to take process notes—there is no process.

3.

Jones wrote that ". . . he did not like being stared at for many hours of the day at close quarters [citing] the necessity for the analyst to be in a position to give free rein to his thoughts without the patient detecting them from the play on his features, which would impair the purity of the transference phenomenon." Jones, op. cit., p.236

COUPLES AT WAR

1.

When seeing one partner in a relationship that is key to resolving the conflict but the other partner refuses to attend a couple's session, I often employ a slightly deceptive tactic. With the participating client's permission, I call the reluctant partner and ask for his or her help in a problem. I say that I am puzzled, baffled by what I have learned from the participating partner, and ask for a meeting with that person as a courtesy to dispel my confusion. In most cases the reluctant partner will agree to come in once, and then I have an opportunity to establish rapport with him or her. If that works, I am free to suggest, firmly, that they come in as a couple. This approach succeeds more often than not.

TARASOFF REVISITED

1.

The so-called duty to protect, meaning protection of a threatened third party, amounts to nothing in real terms. A therapist is not obliged to throw on a cape and knock down the door of the potential victim, a total stranger, shouting, "I'll save you." If the impulse strikes you, shake it off. The justices in Tarasoff, by ruling as they did, gave official proof of the stigma with which many people view the mentally ill—persons such as Poddar. As with most stigmas, this prejudice is based on irrational fear.

REFERENCES

Everstine, L. *The Anatomy of Suicide.* Springfield, Illinois: Charles C. Thomas, 1998.

Everstine, L. *Response: How We Learn.* Bloomington, Indiana: Xlibris, 2011.

Everstine, L., Everstine, D. S., Heymann. G., True, R. H., Frey, D.H., Johnson, H.G., and Seiden, R.H. "Privacy and Confidentiality in Psychotherapy." *American Psychologist 35* (1980): 828–840.

Everstine, D. S. and Everstine, L. *The Trauma Response.* New York: W.W. Norton & Company, 1993.

Everstine, D. S. and Everstine, L. *Strategic Interventions for People in Crisis, Trauma, and Disaster.* New York: Routledge, 2006.

Freud, S. "Analysis Terminable and Interminable." *Int. J. Psycho-Anal. 18*, (1937): 373.

Jones, E. *The Life and Work of Sigmund Freud, vol. 1.* New York: Basic Books, Inc., 1953.

Singer, M. T. and Lolich. J. *Crazy Therapies.* San Francisco: Jossey-Bass Publishers, 1996.

Tarasoff v. Regents of the University of California 17 Cal. 3d 425, 131 Cal. Rptr. 14, 551 P. 2d 334, (1976, 1974).

INDEX

Freud, Sigmund, xv, 1, 8–10
  "Analysis Terminable and
    Interminable," 39–40
friendship, purchase of, 42

H

history, personal, 4, 19

I

improvement, therapeutic, 1
information, 8, 13, 18
interactions, xxi, 35

J

jealousy, 50
Jones, Ernest, 1
judge, 9, 26

L

life, 42
listening, 7, 10
Lolich, Janja, xxii

M

memories, 59
MMPI-2, 17
Moore, Lawrence, 66–68

P

peace, 49
ploys, viii, 73, 75–76
Poddar, Prosenjit, 66–67
police, 71
Powelson, Harvey, 67

privilege, 2, 69
psychiatrists, xx
psychotherapist, 65
psychotherapy, xix, 18

Q

quarrel, 49
questions, probing, 13–14

R

rapport, 1, 5
recovery, 50
relationships, 15, 21, 23
remembering, 22
retaliation, 31

S

science, xix
self, 33
Singer, Margaret, xxii
situation, hypothetical, 15
suicide, 11, 28–29

T

Tarasoff, Tatiana, 65, 68
Tarasoff case, 66
therapeutic practice, doctrines of, xx
therapist, xxi, xxiii–xxiv, 13, 25, 36, 54,
    71–72, 79–81
therapy, xix–xxi, xxiv, 23, 39, 73
  conversation in, 31
  couple's, 45–46, 51
  interactional, 22
  notes in, 11
  supportive, 62

www.ingramcontent.com/pod-product-compliance
Lightning Source LLC
Chambersburg PA
CBHW021545290526
45785CB00004BA/1523